The new baby

Story by Beverley Randell
Illustrated by Ernest Papps

Tom came home after school.

"Hello, Grandpa," he said.
"Where is Mom?
Where is Grandma?"

The new baby

Story by **Beverley Randell**
Illustrated by **Ernest Papps**

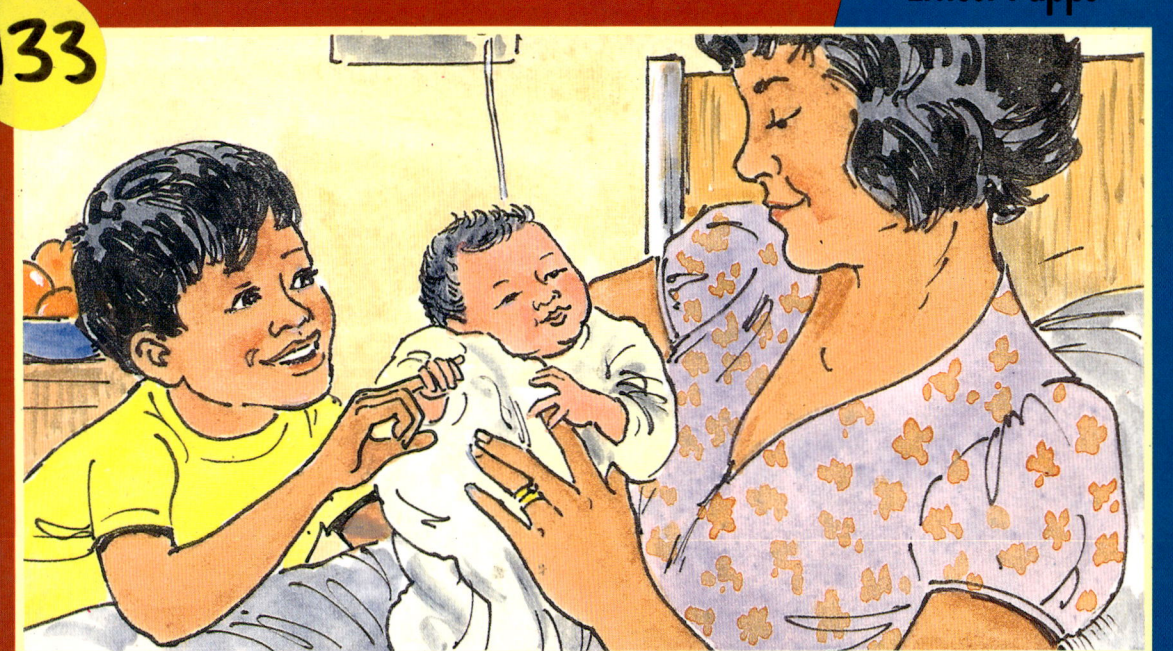

7

Rogers Early Childhood Center
5000 Shenandoah
Allen Park, MI 48101

"Mom is at the hospital,"
said Grandpa.
"The baby is coming.
Dad is with Mom.
Grandma is with Mom, too.
I am staying here with you."

"I am cooking fish,"
said Grandpa.

"I'll help you," said Tom.
"I like cooking."

Tom went to bed. He went to sleep.

Grandpa went to sleep, too.

Ring, ring,
went the phone.

Grandpa woke up.   Tom woke up.

"Hello, hello," said Grandpa.

Grandpa shouted,
"A girl! The baby is a girl!
Baby Emma is here."

Tom shouted,
"A girl! A girl!"

Grandpa and Tom
went to the hospital
to see Mom and Emma.

"I'm going to help you.
I'll take care of Emma, too,"
said Tom.

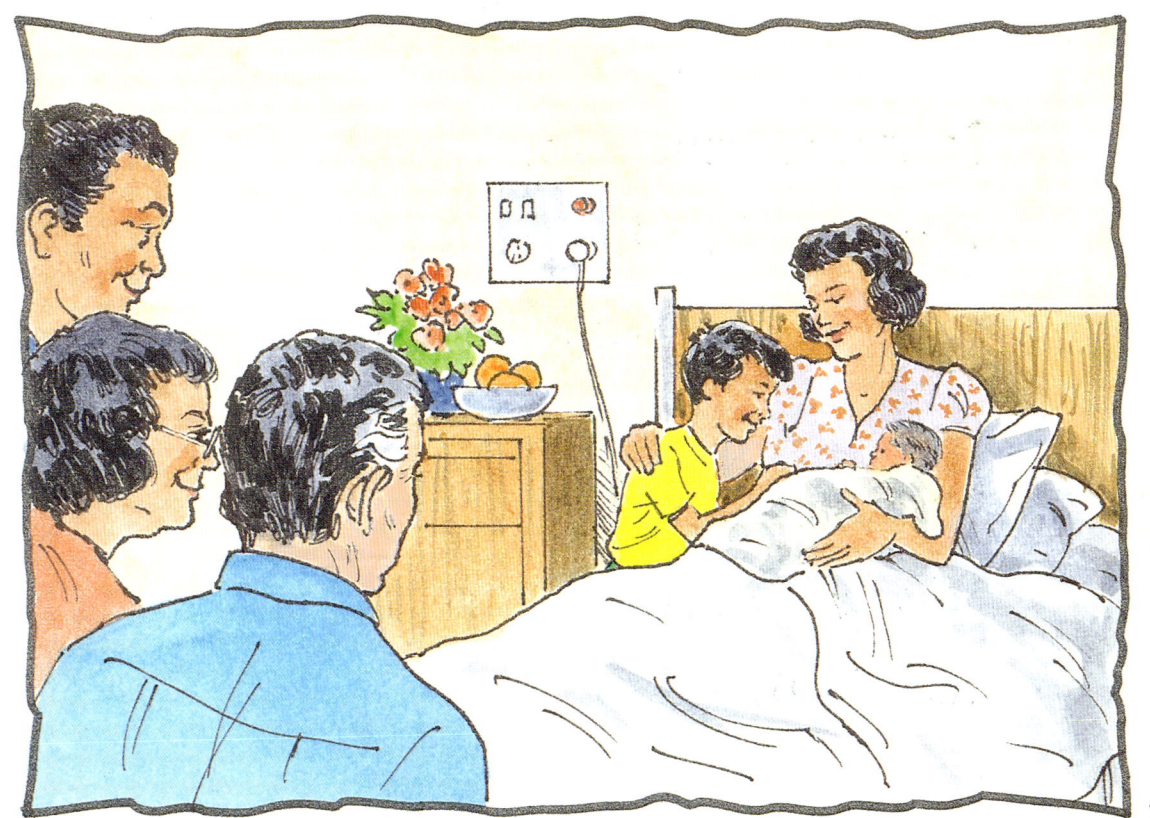

"I like little babies," said Tom.

New PM Story Books
part of the Rigby PM Collection

U.S. edition © 1996 Rigby Education
a division of Reed Elsevier Inc.
1000 Hart Road
Barrington, IL 60010 - 2627

Text © 1994 Beverley Randell
Illustrations © 1994 Nelson Price Milburn

Originally published in New Zealand by Nelson Price Milburn Ltd.

All rights reserved. No part of this publication may be reproduced
or transmitted in any form or by any means, electronic or mechanical,
including photocopying, recording, taping, or any information storage
and retrieval system, without permission in writing from the publisher.

07 06 05 04 03 02 01
18 17 16 15 14 13

The new baby
ISBN 0-4350-6695-1

Printed in China by Midas Printing (Asia) Ltd.

NEW PM STORY BOOKS